fox

Contents

skunk

dog

D1118532

How to Make Paper Tube Animals

Follow these basic steps for each of the animals in Paper Tube Zoo.

Prepare the Tube

Cover the tube in the appropriate colored construction paper.

1. Cut the paper 4½" x 6" (11.5 cm x 16.5 cm).

2. Tape one end of the paper to the paper tube.

3. Roll the paper around the tube and place tape along the end flap.

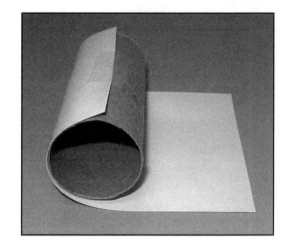

Complete the Animal

1. Cut out the pattern pieces.
If the pieces are reproduced on colored paper, just cut them out. If the pieces have been reproduced on white paper, you have two choices:

• Color the pieces with crayons or marking pens.

• Use the pieces as templates. Cut out the patterns. Lay them on colored paper and trace around them. Cut out the colored pieces.

2. Glue the pieces to the covered tube as shown on the pattern page for each animal.

How To Use Paper Tube Animals

Writing

A reproducible form is provided for each animal. It presents a poem about the animal, and provides a place to set the completed animal and lines for writing a story or report about it.

Use the animal characters to motivate students to write

- original stories,
- nonfiction reports, and
- poetry
- descriptive words
- animal facts

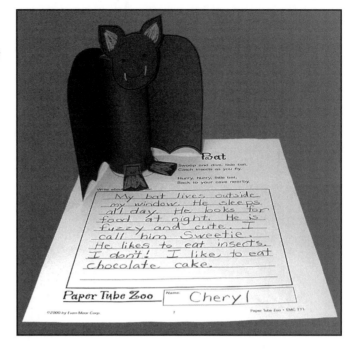

Puppets

- Use the paper tube characters in telling original stories or for retelling a favorite piece of literature.
- The animals can be used as finger puppets (set the tube over two or three fingers).
- They may be used as stick puppets (tape the tube to the end of a ruler).

Bulletin Board Displays

- Pin the characters in a line to create a colorful border for a display of student work related to animals.
- Pin the characters to a bulletin board along with student reports about animals.

Desk Companion

Tape the paper tube characters to students' desks to hold pencils, flash cards, sentence strips, or a special treat on students' birthdays.

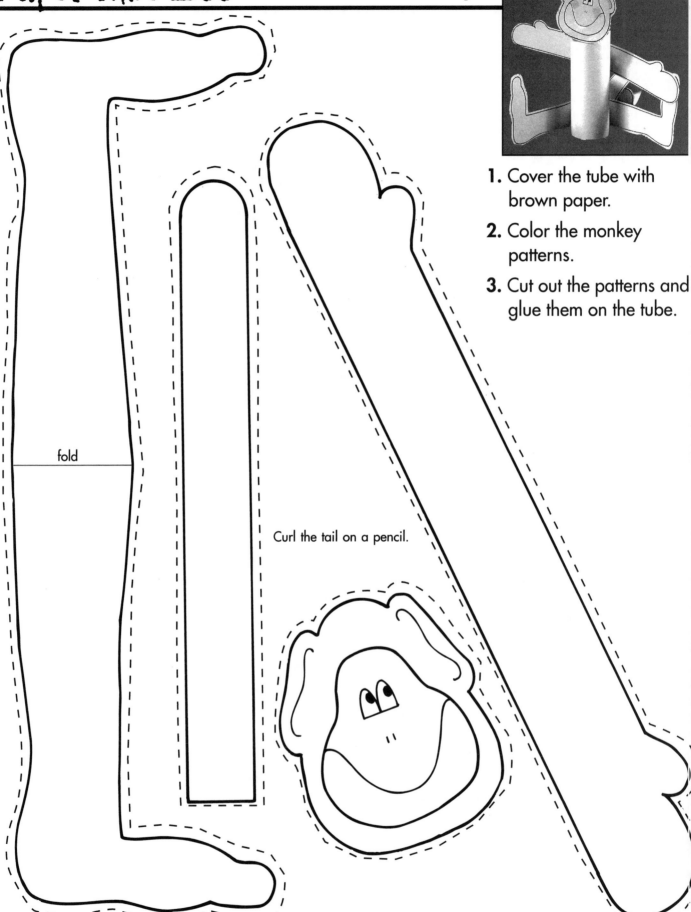

1. Cover the tube with brown paper.

2. Color the monkey patterns.

3. Cut out the patterns and glue them on the tube.

fold

Curl the tail on a pencil.

Place your
Paper Tube Zoo
friend here.

Monkey

Wouldn't it be fun to be
Monkeys swinging tree to tree?

Write about your animal.

_____

_____

_____

_____

_____

_____

_____

_____

Paper Tube Zoo

Name:

Paper Tube Zoo

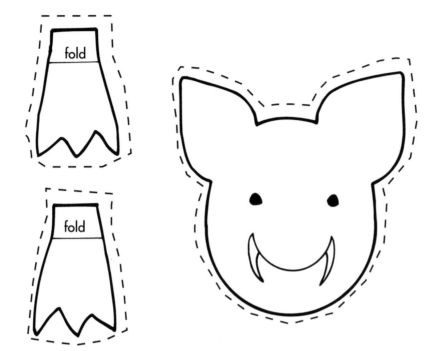

1. Cover the tube with black paper.

2. Color the bat patterns.

3. Cut out the patterns and glue them on the tube.

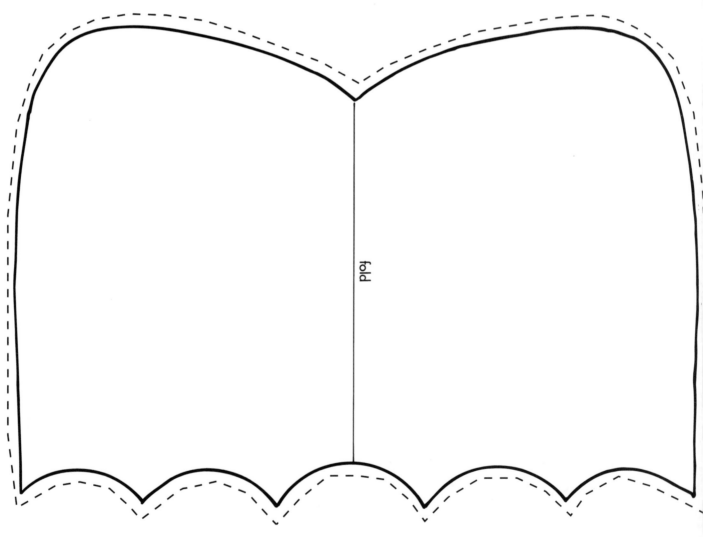

Paper Tube Zoo • EMC 771

Place your
Paper Tube Zoo
friend here.

Bat

Swoop and dive, little bat,
Catch insects as you fly.

Hurry, hurry, little bat,
Back to your cave nearby.

Write about your animal.

_____

_____

_____

_____

_____

_____

_____

_____

Paper Tube Zoo

Name:

Paper Tube Zoo

Beaver

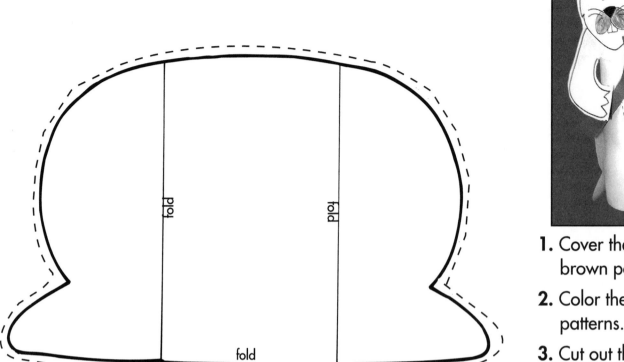

1. Cover the tube with brown paper.

2. Color the beaver patterns.

3. Cut out the patterns and glue them on the tube.

fold

fold

fold

cut

Paper Tube Zoo • EMC 771

Beaver

Place your
Paper Tube Zoo
friend here.

Busy beaver is quite skilled.
You should see what it can build.

Write about your animal.

Paper Tube Zoo

Name:

Bear

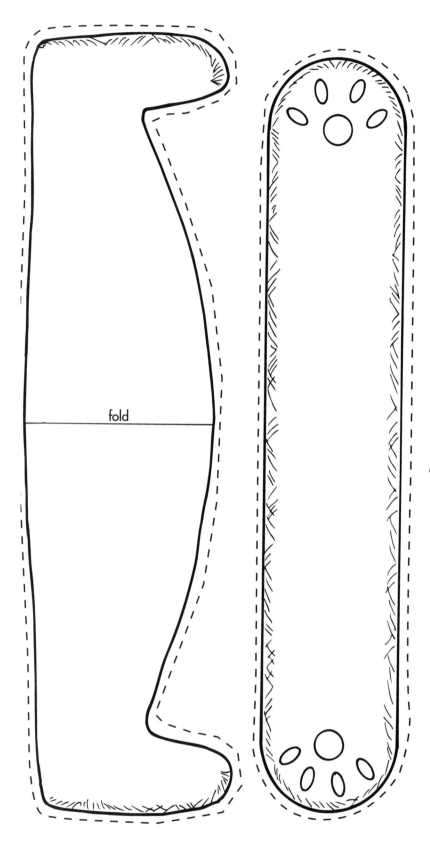

1. Cover the tube with brown paper.

2. Color the bear patterns.

3. Cut out the patterns and glue them on the tube.

fold

glue

Place your
Paper Tube Zoo
friend here.

Bear

Bear sleeps through the winter
Then awakes in the spring.

Bear wakes up so hungry
He'll eat most anything.

Write about your animal.

Paper Tube Zoo

Name:

Pig

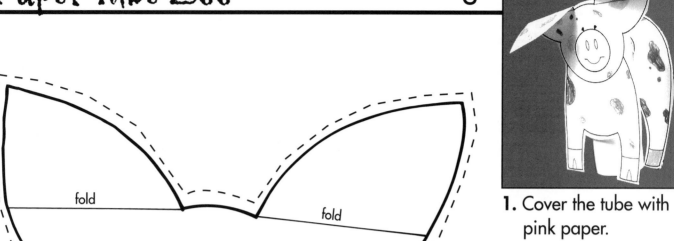

1. Cover the tube with pink paper.
2. Color the pig patterns.
3. Cut out the patterns and glue them on the tube.

fold   fold

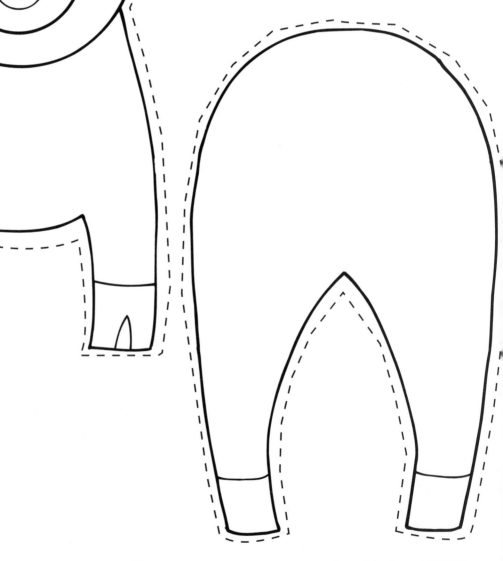

Place your
Paper Tube Zoo
friend here.

Pig

Curly tail and muddy snout,
Feed the pig and let it out.

Write about your animal.

_____

_____

_____

_____

_____

_____

_____

_____

Paper Tube Zoo

Name:

Paper Tube Zoo

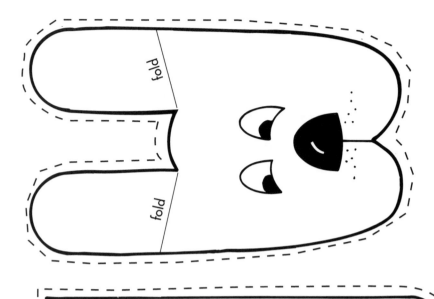

1. Cover the tube with paper.

2. Color the dog patterns.

3. Cut out the patterns and glue them on the tube.

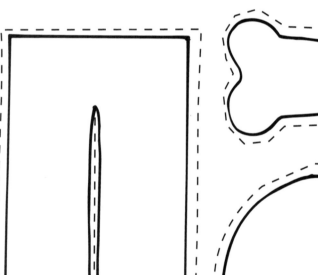

fold   fold

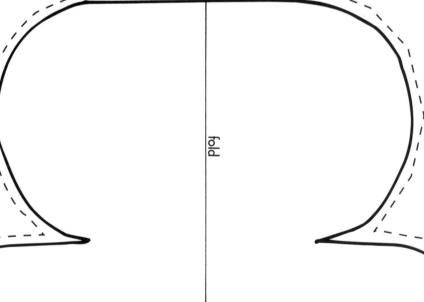

fold

Place your
Paper Tube Zoo
friend here.

Dog

Wag, beg, bark, and lick.
Run, dig, fetch a stick.

That's my pup!

Write about your animal.

_____

_____

_____

_____

_____

_____

_____

_____

Paper Tube Zoo

Name:

Paper Tube Zoo • EMC 771

Paper Tube Zoo

Koala

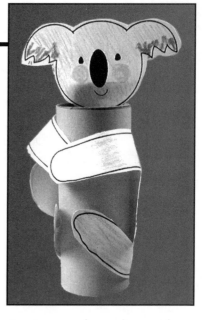

1. Cover the tube with brown paper.

2. Color the koala patterns.

3. Cut out the patterns and glue them on the tube.

Wrap the arms around the tube.

fold

16

Koala

Place your
Paper Tube Zoo
friend here.

Koala sits there in the tree,
Eats a leaf, and looks at me.

Write about your animal.

Paper Tube Zoo

Name:

Mouse

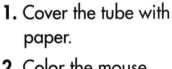

1. Cover the tube with paper.

2. Color the mouse patterns.

3. Cut out the patterns and glue them on the tube.

Curl the tail on a pencil.

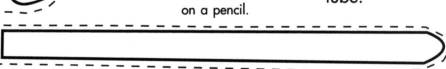

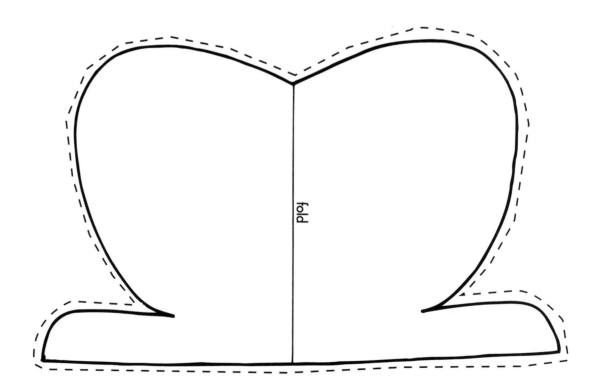

fold

Place your
Paper Tube Zoo
friend here.

Mouse

Bright eyes shine
in a furry face.
Tiny feet scurry
from place to place.

Write about your animal.

_____

_____

_____

_____

_____

_____

_____

_____

Paper Tube Zoo

Name:

Paper Tube Zoo

beak

wings

Glue the folded
beak on the duck's
head.

fold

1. **Cover the tube with paper.**
2. **Color the duck patterns.**
3. **Cut out the patterns and glue them on the tube.**

tail

fold

fold

fold

fold

Paper Tube Zoo • EMC 771

Place your
Paper Tube Zoo
friend here.

Duck

Can you see me waddle?
Can you hear me quack?
I'm a little duck with
feathers on my back.

Write about your animal.

Paper Tube Zoo

Name:

Paper Tube Zoo

Cat

1. Cover the tube with paper.

2. Color the cat patterns.

3. Cut out the patterns and glue them on the tube.

Curl the tail on a pencil.

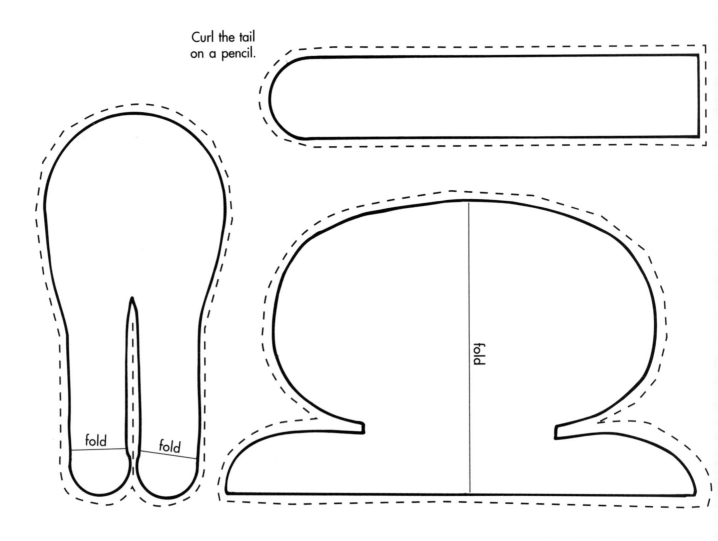

fold

fold

fold

Place your
Paper Tube Zoo
friend here.

Cat

Little kitten, sit with me.
Rest your head here on my knee.
Let me scratch your velvet ear
While you get your purr in gear.

Write about your animal.

Paper Tube Zoo

Name:

Paper Tube Zoo

Cow

1. Cover the tube with brown paper.
2. Color the cow patterns.
3. Cut out the patterns and glue them on the tube.

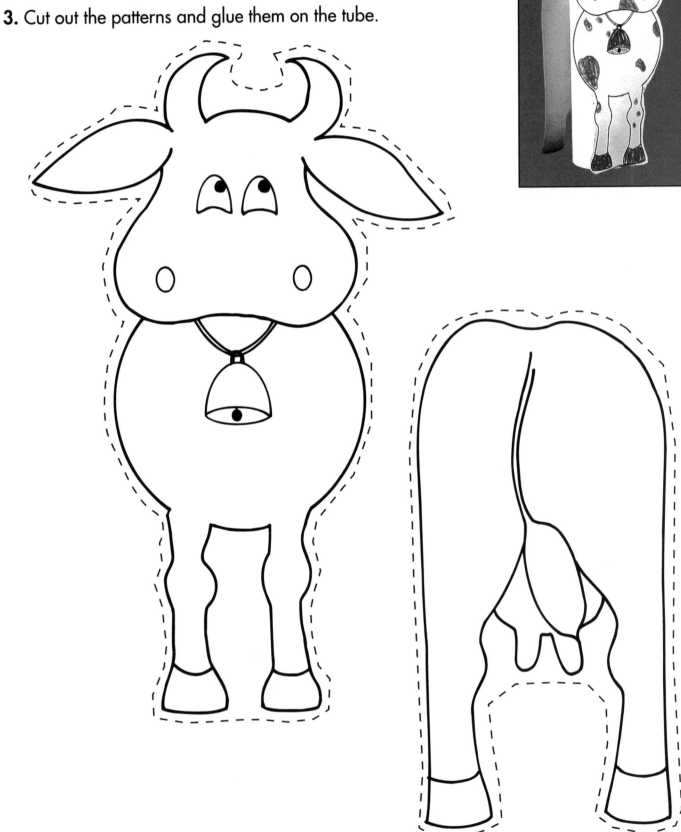

Place your
Paper Tube Zoo
friend here.

Cow

My cow eats grass,
Chewing over and over.
She's making milk
From all that tasty clover.

Write about your animal.

Paper Tube Zoo

Name:

Paper Tube Zoo

1. Cover the tube with yellow paper.

2. Color the lion patterns.

3. Cut out the patterns and glue them on the tube.

cut

fold   fold

Curl the tail on a pencil.

fold

Place your
Paper Tube Zoo
friend here.

Lion

If I were a lion
I'd roar and roar and roar.
I'd show my teeth and claws
Then chase you out the door!

Write about your animal.

_____

_____

_____

_____

_____

_____

_____

_____

Paper Tube Zoo

Name:

Paper Tube Zoo

Frog

1. Cover the tube with green paper.

2. Color the frog patterns.

3. Cut out the patterns and glue them on the tube.

Glue the legs to the side of the tube.

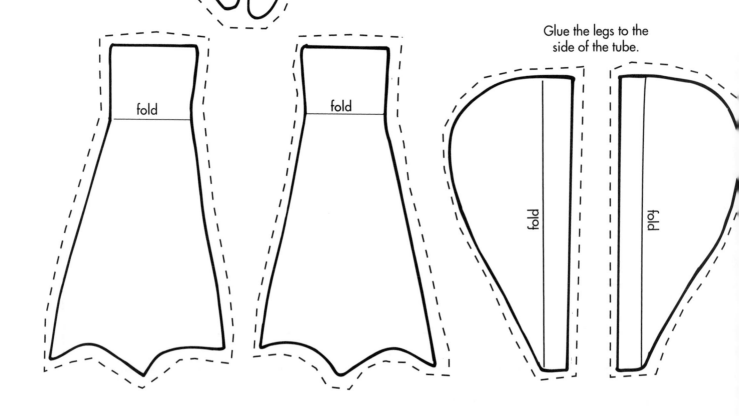

fold

fold

fold

fold

Place your
Paper Tube Zoo
friend here.

Frog

Its webbed feet swim.
Its strong legs hop.
Carrying frog
From spot to spot.

Write about your animal.

_____

_____

_____

_____

_____

_____

_____

_____

Paper Tube Zoo

Name:

Paper Tube Zoo • EMC 771

Paper Tube Zoo

Lamb

1. Cover the tube with paper.
2. Color the lamb patterns.
3. Cut out the patterns and glue them on the tube.

Place your
Paper Tube Zoo
friend here.

Lamb

Lamb wears a curly, woolly coat
All furry from its tail to throat.

Lamb takes it off just once a year
When it gets its summer shear.

Write about your animal.

_____

_____

_____

_____

_____

_____

_____

_____

Paper Tube Zoo

Name:

Paper Tube Zoo

1. Cover the tube with paper.

2. Color the bunny patterns.

3. Cut out the patterns and glue them on the tube.

4. Glue a cotton ball on the back of the tube for a tail.

cut

fold   fold

Place your
Paper Tube Zoo
friend here.

Bunny

Bunny twitches its nose.
Bunny turns its long ears.
Bunny sees a carrot.
The carrot disappears.

Write about your animal.

_____

_____

_____

_____

_____

_____

_____

_____

Paper Tube Zoo

Name:

Paper Tube Zoo   Penguin

1. Cover the tube with black paper.

2. Color the penguin patterns.

3. Cut out the patterns and glue them on the tube.

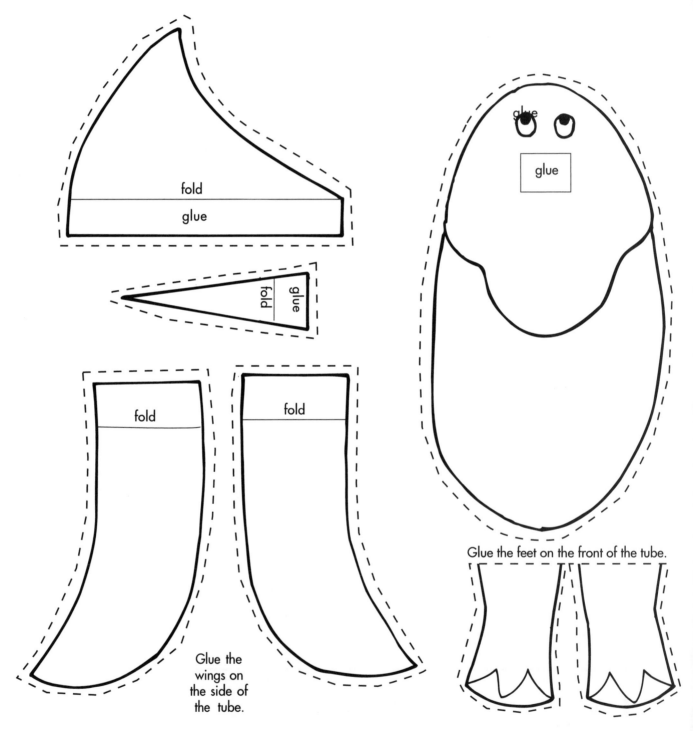

fold

glue

glue

fold

glue

glue

fold

fold

Glue the feet on the front of the tube.

Glue the wings on the side of the tube.

Place your
Paper Tube Zoo
friend here.

Penguin

Dressed all in feathers
Of black and of white,
The penguin's a bird
That never takes flight.

Write about your animal.

Paper Tube Zoo

Name:

35

Paper Tube Zoo

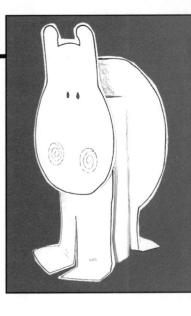

1. Cover the tube with paper.

2. Color the hippo patterns.

3. Cut out the patterns and glue them on the tube.

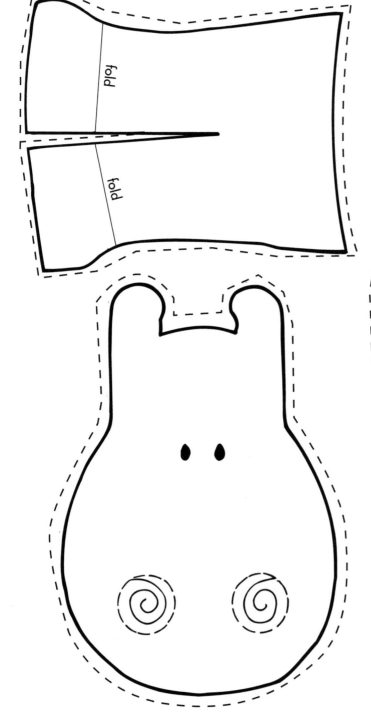

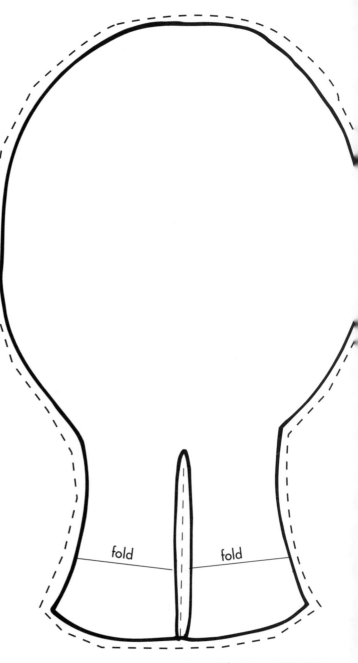

Place your
Paper Tube Zoo
friend here.

Hippo

Hippo can be found
Floating round and round.
Ears and eyes and nose
Are all that hippo shows.

Write about your animal.

Paper Tube Zoo

Name:

Paper Tube Zoo

Toucan

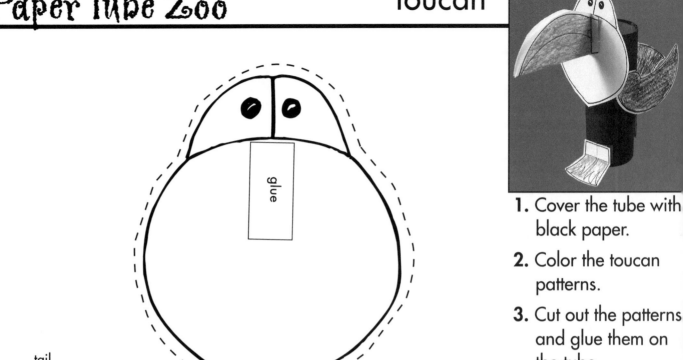

1. Cover the tube with black paper.
2. Color the toucan patterns.
3. Cut out the patterns and glue them on the tube.

glue

tail

beak

fold fold

fold

feet

Glue the wings to the side of the tube.

Place your
Paper Tube Zoo
friend here.

Toucan

With bright feathers
And a huge beak,
Toucan's a bird
That's quite unique.

Write about your animal.

Paper Tube Zoo

Name:

Paper Tube Zoo

1. Cover the tube with black paper.

2. Color the skunk patterns.

3. Cut out the patterns and glue them on the tube.

fold

fold

glue

Place your
Paper Tube Zoo
friend here.

Skunk

Skunk has a stripe
From its head to its tail.
Skunk squirts an odor
You won't want to smell!

Write about your animal.

_____

_____

_____

_____

_____

_____

_____

_____

Paper Tube Zoo

Name:

Paper Tube Zoo

Walrus

1. Cover the tube with brown paper.
2. Color the walrus patterns.
3. Cut out the patterns and glue them on the tube.

Paper Tube Zoo • EMC 771

Place your
Paper Tube Zoo
friend here.

Walrus

A walrus is
    a remarkable beast
With whiskers and tusks
    to dig up a feast.

Write about your animal.

_____

_____

_____

_____

_____

_____

_____

_____

_____

Paper Tube Zoo

Name:

 Paper Tube Zoo • EMC 771

Paper Tube Zoo

Fox

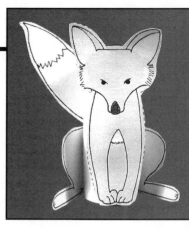

1. Cover the tube with red paper.

2. Color the fox patterns.

3. Cut out the patterns and glue them on the tube.

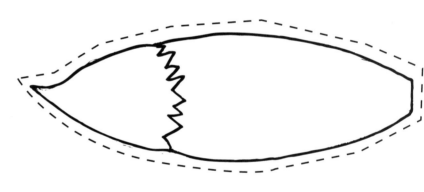

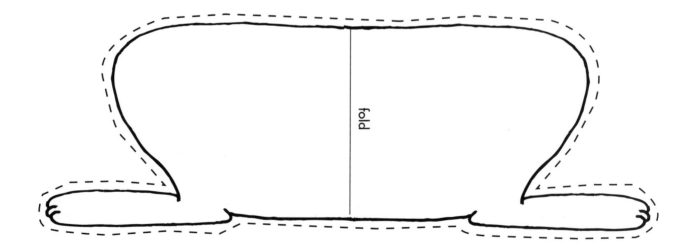

fold

Paper Tube Zoo • EMC 771

Place your
Paper Tube Zoo
friend here.

Fox

Big bushy tail and pointy nose,
Fox is clever, as anyone knows.

Write about your animal.

_____

_____

_____

_____

_____

_____

_____

_____

_____

Paper Tube Zoo

Name:

Paper Tube Zoo

Turkey

fold

fold

glue

1. Cover the tube with brown paper.

2. Color the turkey patterns.

3. Cut out the patterns and glue them on the tube.

Paper Tube Zoo • EMC 771

Place your
Paper Tube Zoo
friend here.

Turkey

Turkey, turkey, spread your tail—
Gobble and strut about the farm.
Turkey, turkey, all is well—
No one means you any harm.

Write about your animal.

_____

_____

_____

_____

_____

_____

_____

_____

_____

Paper Tube Zoo

Name:

Paper Tube Zoo

Octopus

1. Cover the tube with paper.

2. Color the octopus patterns.

3. Cut out the patterns and glue them on the tube.

glue inside tube

fold

glue inside tube

fold inside tube

fold

cut cut cut cut cut cut cut

Place your
Paper Tube Zoo
friend here.

Octopus

Octopus squirts a cloud of ink
To make attackers stop and think!

Write about your animal.

_____

_____

_____

_____

_____

_____

_____

_____

_____

Paper Tube Zoo

Name:

Paper Tube Zoo • EMC 771

Paper Tube Zoo

Goat

1. Cover the tube with white paper.
2. Color the goat patterns.
3. Cut out the patterns and glue them on the tube.

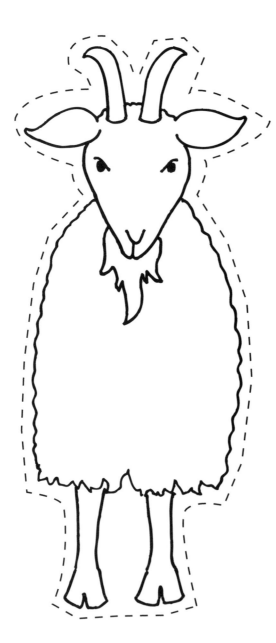

Paper Tube Zoo • EMC 771

Place your
Paper Tube Zoo
friend here.

Goat

Nanny goat's the mother.
Billy goat's the dad.
And this little fellow
Is the kid they had.

Write about your animal.

Paper Tube Zoo

Name:

Paper Tube Zoo

Chicken

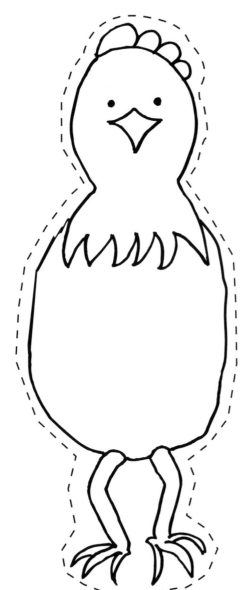

1. Cover the tube with green paper.

2. Color the hen and chick patterns.

3. Cut out the patterns and glue them on the tube.

wings

52

Place your
Paper Tube Zoo
friend here.

Chicken

Mother Hen is on her nest,
Feathers fluffed about her legs.
She is having a good rest,
As she sits upon her eggs.

Write about your animal.

_____

_____

_____

_____

_____

_____

_____

_____

Paper Tube Zoo

Name:

Panda

1. Cover the tube with white paper.

2. Color the panda patterns.

3. Cut out the patterns and glue them on the tube.

Cut open and slip over tube.

Glue bamboo in panda's paw.

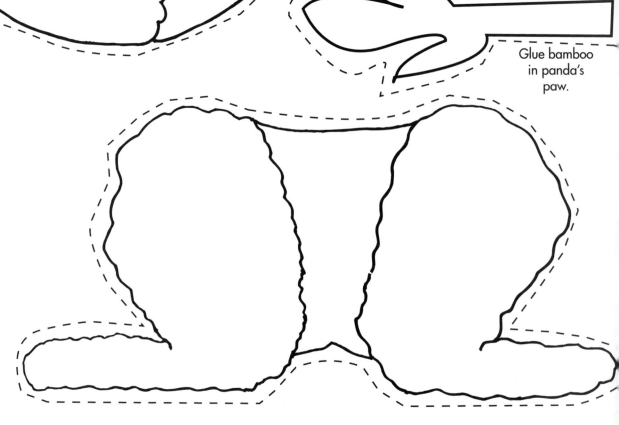

Place your
Paper Tube Zoo
friend here.

Panda

Giant panda all black and white.
Looks for bamboo that tastes just right.

It nibbles on the leaves and shoots
Then digs around for tasty roots.

Write about your animal.

_____

_____

_____

_____

_____

_____

_____

_____

_____

Paper Tube Zoo

Name:

Paper Tube Zoo

Raccoon

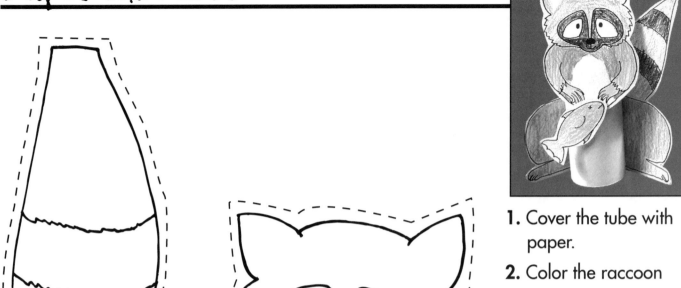

1. Cover the tube with paper.
2. Color the raccoon patterns.
3. Cut out the patterns and glue them on the tube.

fold

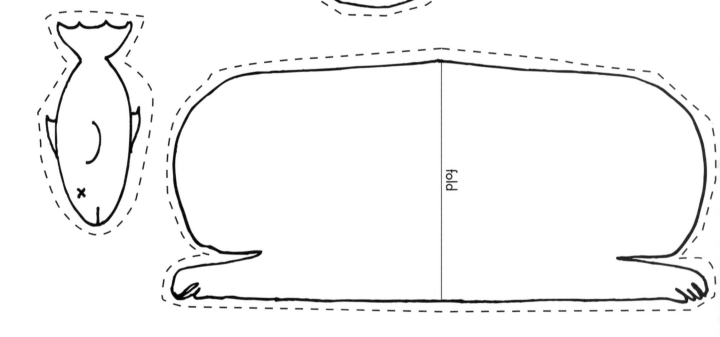

Paper Tube Zoo • EMC 771

Raccoon

Place your
Paper Tube Zoo
friend here.

There's a big raccoon in my neighborhood.
He looks mighty cute, but he's not very good.

He dumps all the garbage he can find.
That naughty raccoon leaves a mess behind!

Write about your animal.

_____

_____

_____

_____

_____

_____

_____

_____

_____

Paper Tube Zoo

Name:

Paper Tube Zoo

1. Cover the tube with brown paper.

2. Color the owl patterns.

3. Cut out the patterns and glue them on the tube.

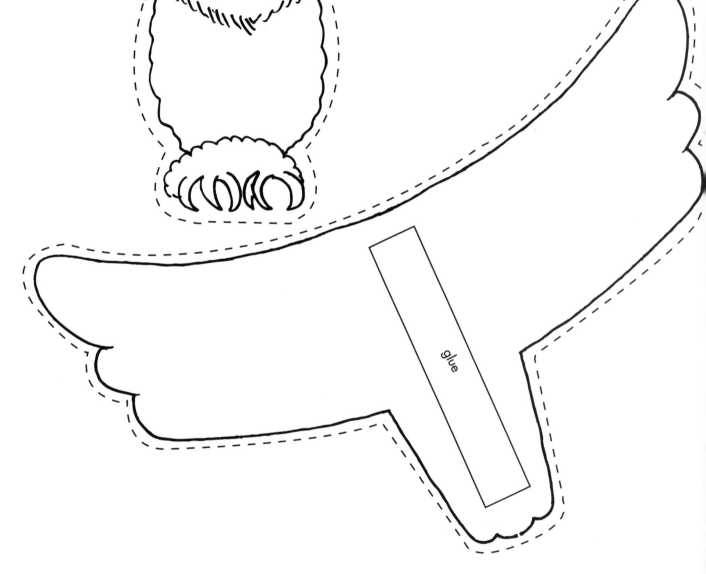

glue

Place your
Paper Tube Zoo
friend here.

Owl

Silent hunter of the night,
Owl will sleep when it is light.

Write about your animal.

_____

_____

_____

_____

_____

_____

_____

Paper Tube Zoo

Name:

Paper Tube Zoo

Snake

1. Cover the tube with paper.
2. Color the snake pattern.
3. Cut out the pattern and wrap it around the tube. Glue it in place.

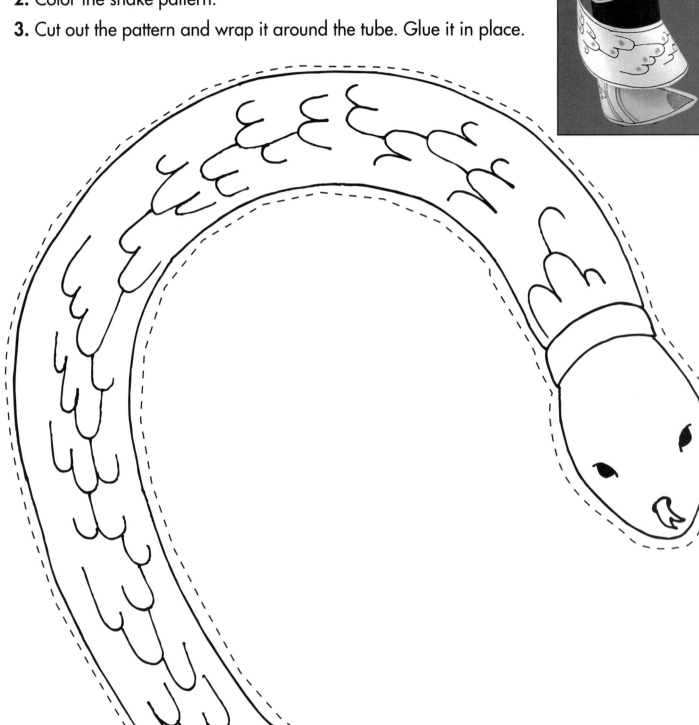

Place your
Paper Tube Zoo
friend here.

Snake

A snake has scales,
two eyes, and a nose.
But it is missing
legs, arms, and toes.

Write about your animal.

Paper Tube Zoo

Name:

Paper Tube Zoo • EMC 771

Paper Tube Zoo

Butterfly

1. Cover the tube with black paper.

2. Color the butterfly patterns.

3. Cut out the patterns and glue them on the tube.

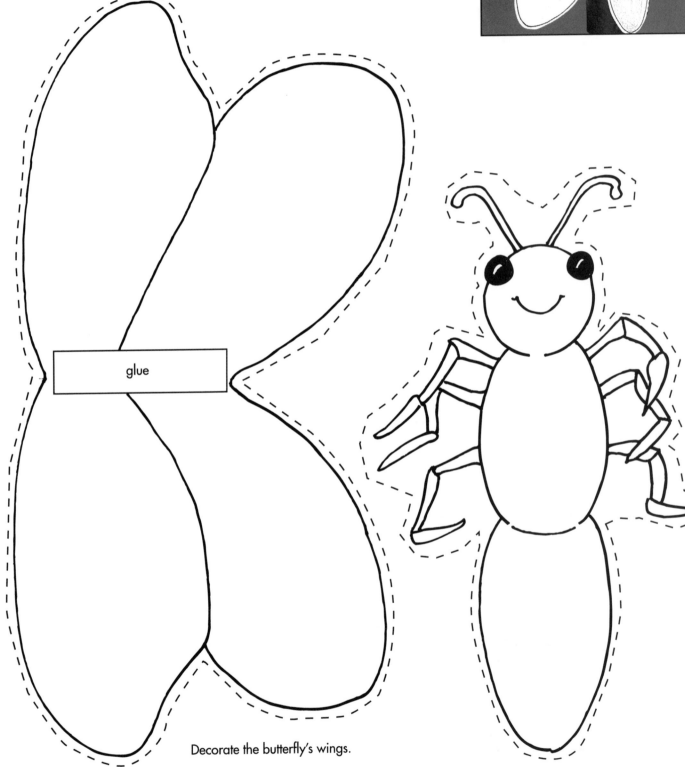

glue

Decorate the butterfly's wings.

Place your
Paper Tube Zoo
friend here.

Butterfly

Flutter by, butterfly,
On silent wing.

Flutter by, butterfly,
Come in the spring.

Write about your animal.

_____

_____

_____

_____

_____

_____

_____

_____

Paper Tube Zoo

Name:

Paper Tube Zoo

Bumblebee

1. Cover the tube with black paper.
2. Color the bee patterns.
3. Cut out the patterns and glue them on the tube.

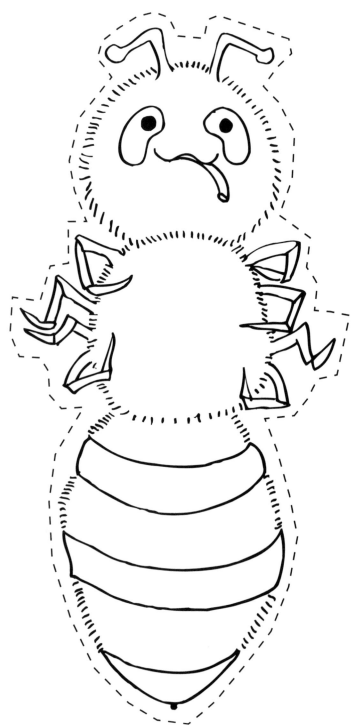

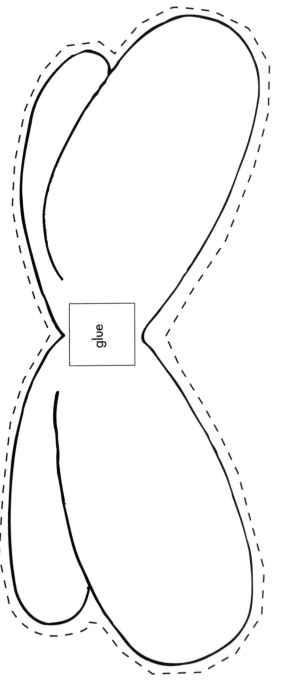

glue

Paper Tube Zoo • EMC 771

Place your
Paper Tube Zoo
friend here.

Bumblebee

Did you know that bumblebees
Are round and fat and fuzzy?
Have you seen bumblebees
So busy and so buzzy?

Write about your animal.

_____

_____

_____

_____

_____

_____

_____

_____

Paper Tube Zoo

Name:

Elephant

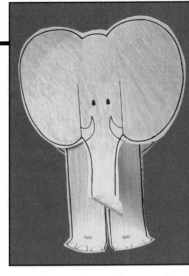

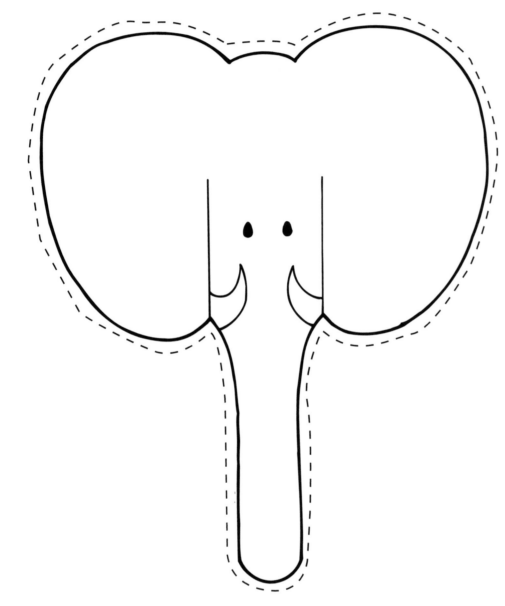

1. **Cover the tube with gray paper.**

2. **Color the elephant patterns.**

3. **Cut out the patterns and glue them on the tube.**

Color both sides of the trunk and curl it on a pencil.

Paper Tube Zoo • EMC 771

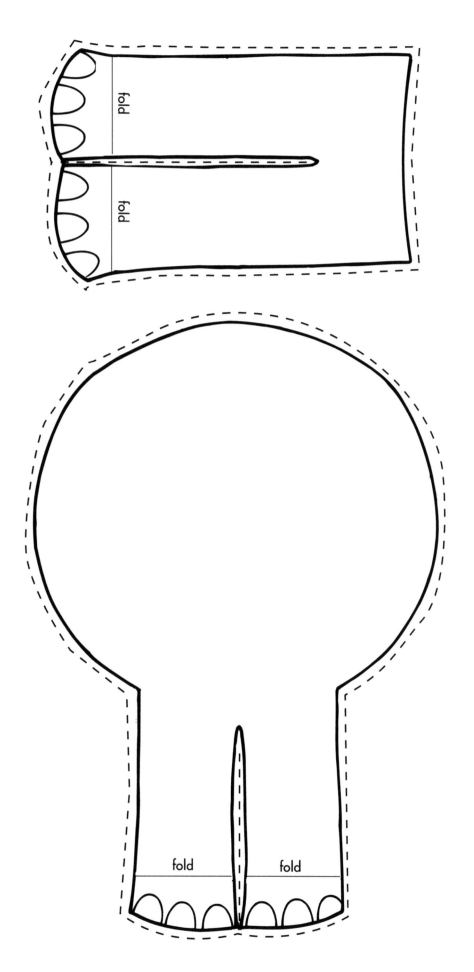

fold

fold

fold   fold

Place your
Paper Tube Zoo
friend here.

Elephant

Gray,
   saggy,
      baggy
         skin.
That's the cover an elephant's in.

Write about your animal.

Paper Tube Zoo

Name:

Paper Tube Zoo

Kangaroo

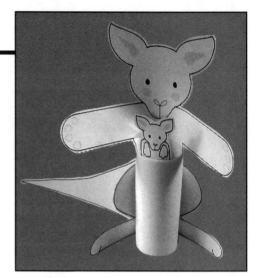

1. Cover the tube with brown paper.
2. Color the kangaroo patterns.
3. Cut out the patterns and glue them on the tube.

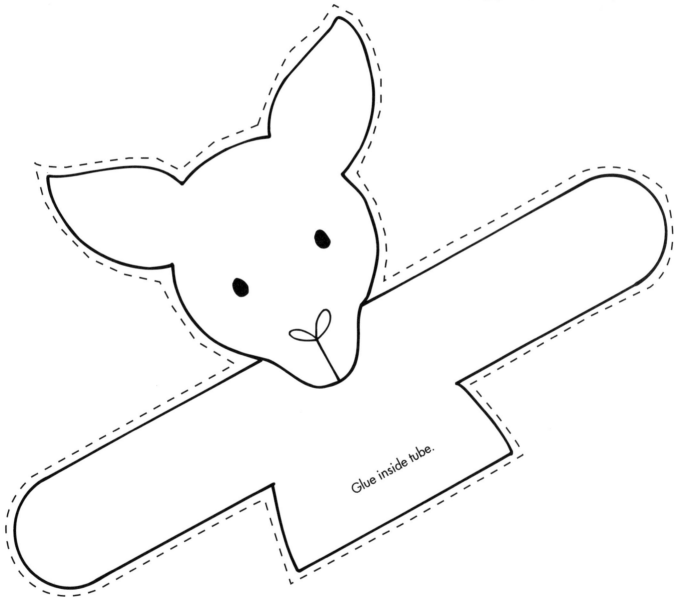

Glue inside tube.

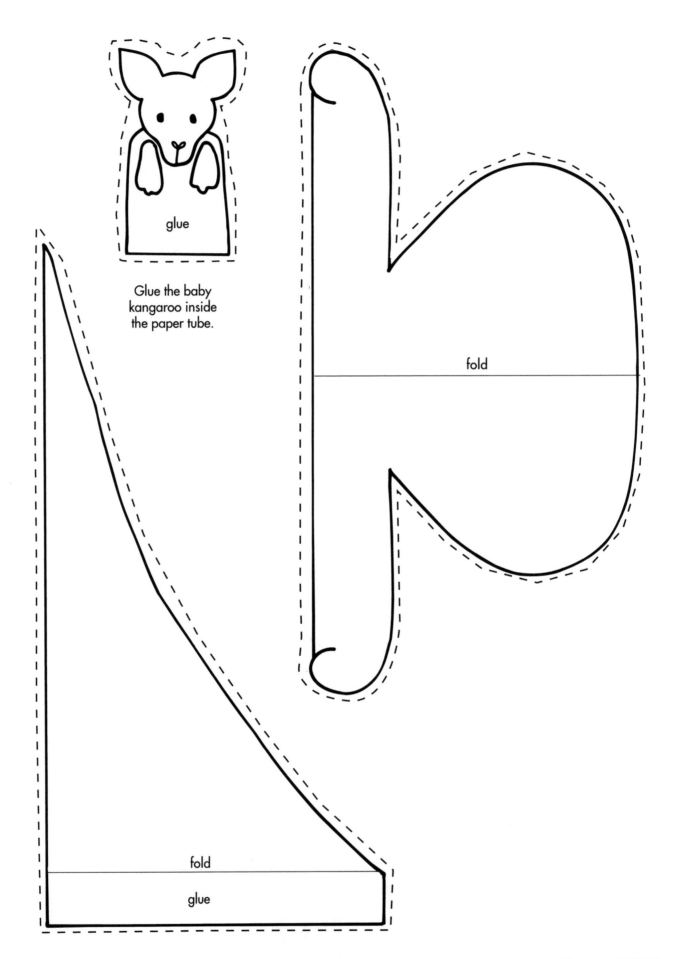

glue

Glue the baby
kangaroo inside
the paper tube.

fold

fold

glue

Kangaroo

Place your
Paper Tube Zoo
friend here.

Mother Kangaroo has a small surprise
Hiding in her pouch away from watching eyes.

A teeny, tiny joey growing day by day,
Sleeping and eating 'til it's big enough to play.

Write about your animal.

_____

_____

_____

_____

_____

_____

_____

_____

Paper Tube Zoo

Name:

Paper Tube Zoo

Squirrel

1. Cover the tube with paper.
2. Color the squirrel patterns.
3. Cut out the patterns and glue them on the tube.

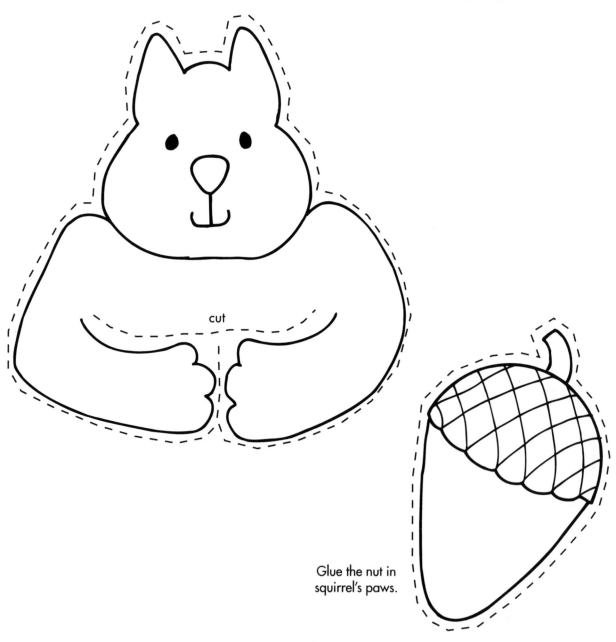

cut

Glue the nut in
squirrel's paws.

Paper Tube Zoo • EMC 771

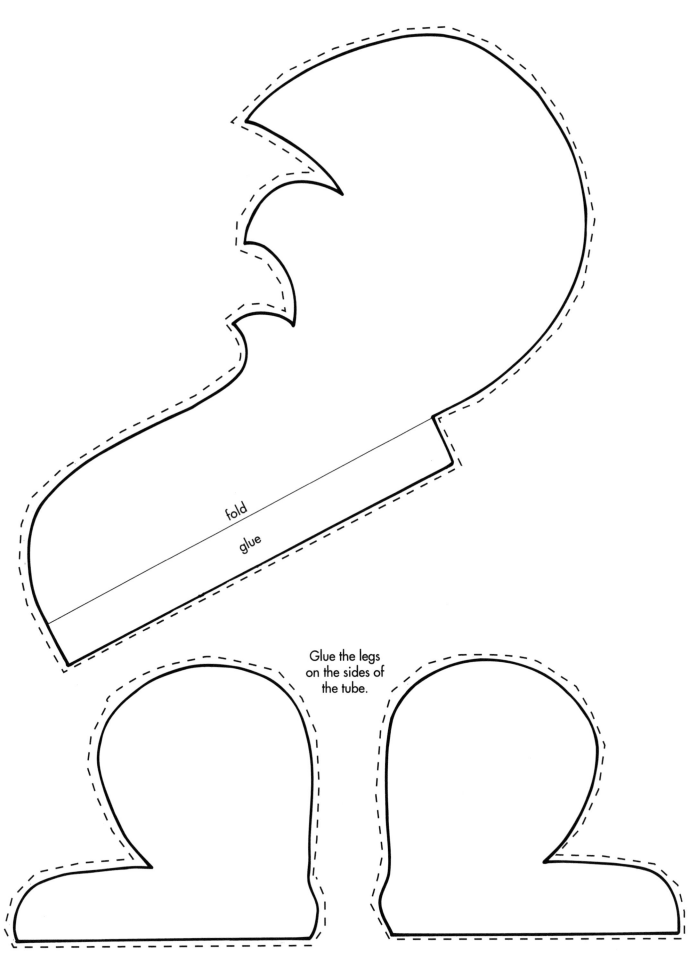

fold

glue

Glue the legs
on the sides of
the tube.

Place your
Paper Tube Zoo
friend here.

Squirrel

Forest explored.
Food found and stored.
Squirrel is ready for winter.

Write about your animal.

_____

_____

_____

_____

_____

_____

_____

_____

Paper Tube Zoo

Name:

Paper Tube Zoo

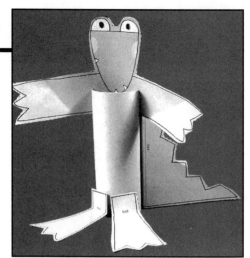

1. Cover the tube with green paper.
2. Color the crocodile patterns.
3. Cut out the patterns and glue them on the tube.

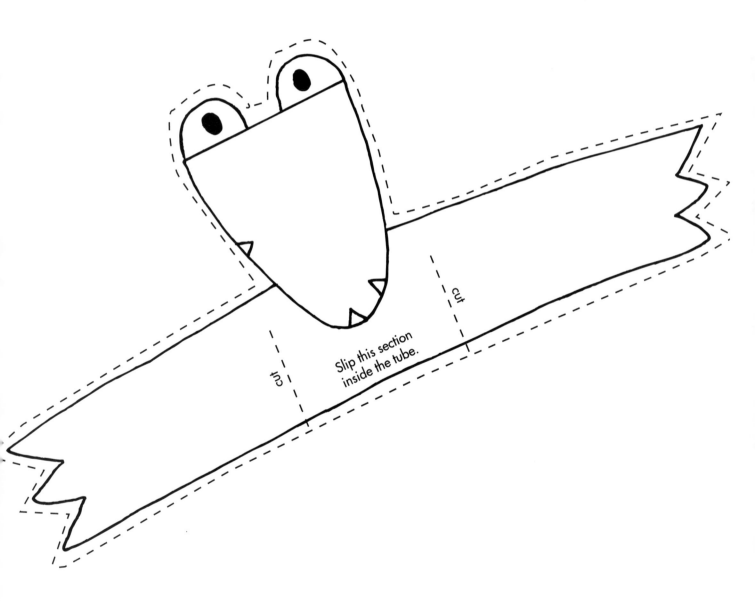

cut

cut

Slip this section inside the tube.

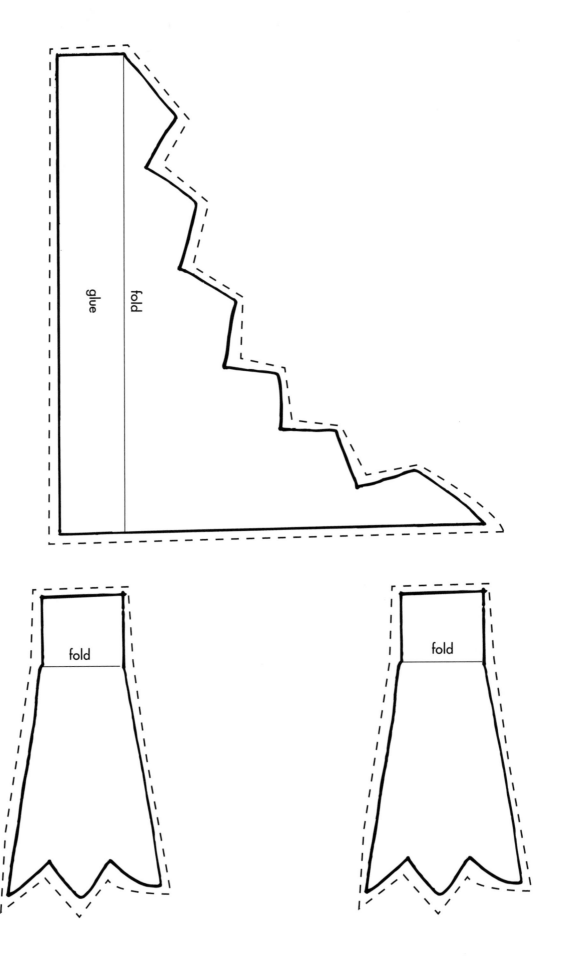

glue

fold

fold

fold

Place your
Paper Tube Zoo
friend here.

Crocodile

Alligator has a broad, broad nose.
Crocodile's is thin.
But both of them are dangerous
When they begin to grin.

Write about your animal.

Paper Tube Zoo

Name:

Paper Tube Zoo

Pony

1. Cover the tube with paper.
2. Color the pony patterns.
3. Cut out the patterns and glue them on the tube.

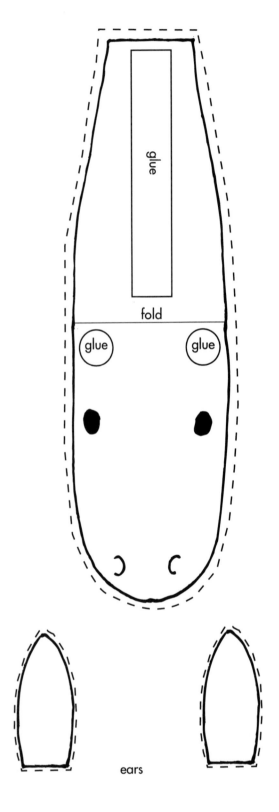

glue

fold

glue   glue

ears

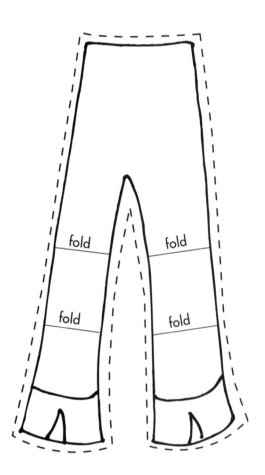

fold   fold

fold   fold

Paper Tube Zoo • EMC 771

mane

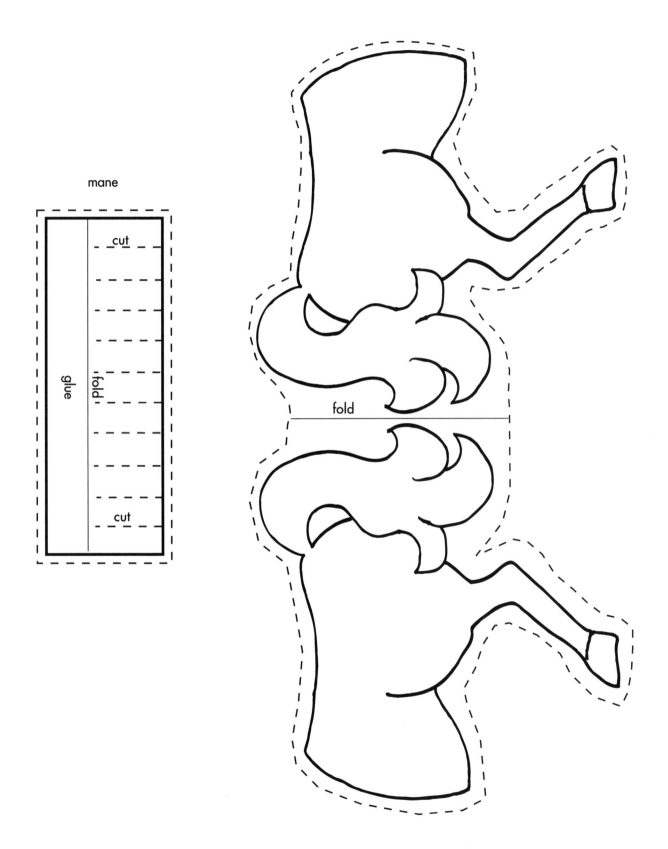

cut

glue fold

cut

fold

Place your
Paper Tube Zoo
friend here.

Pony

I have a little pony.
I ride upon his back,
We hurry to the stable
To get his tasty snack.

Write about your animal.

Paper Tube Zoo

Name: